AuthorHouse™
1663 Liberty Drive
Bloomington, IN 47403
www.authorhouse.com
Phone: 1 (800) 839-8640

Published by AuthorHouse 11/28/2016

ISBN: 978-1-5246-4449-9 (sc)
ISBN: 978-1-5246-4448-2 (e)
ISBN: 978-1-5246-4744-5 (h)

Library of Congress Control Number: 2016916844

Print information available on the last page.

This book is printed on acid-free paper.

authorHOUSE®

The Kitten from Great Britain

Written by Chris Cash

Illustrated by Eric Baca

First Edition

For Taylor & Mom
- Chris Cash

For Kiley & Maxon
- Eric Baca

Special thanks to Jennifer, Jordin, and Henry Daut

The Kitten from Great Britain loves making new friends

especially when those friends are from all around the world

The
Crane from Spain
enjoys flying her
around the world
like a plane

Mornings are spent doing yoga in togas with the Geese from Greece

Another thing she loves
to do is fly kites with the
Caribou from Peru

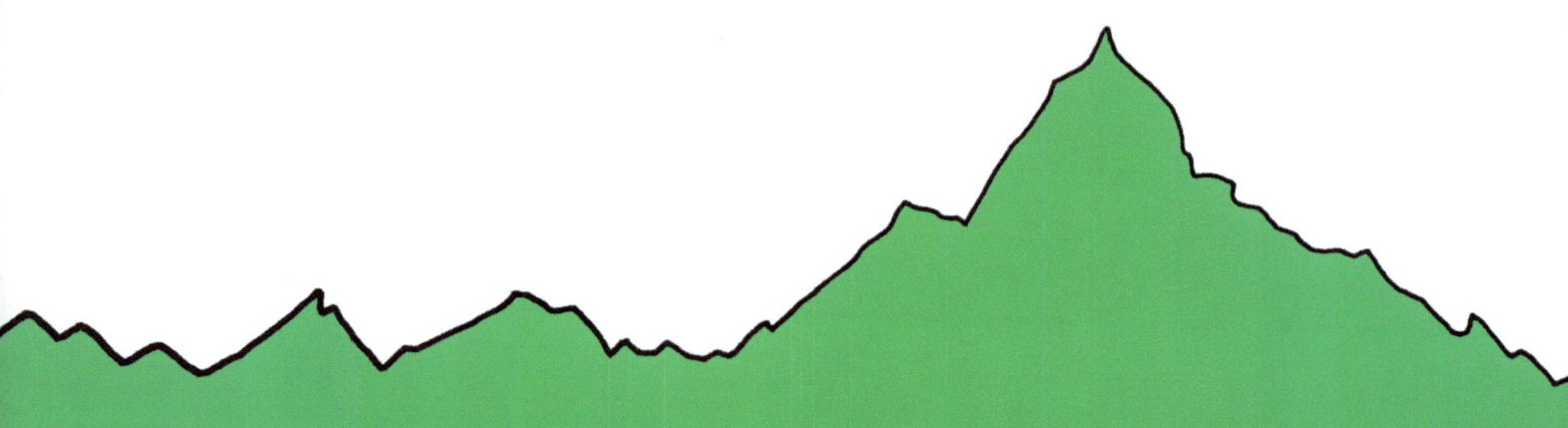

The Kitten from Great Britain loves to munch on lunch with the Lamb from Pakistan

She always finds time to prance around France with the Crow from Bordeaux

She glides down
slides with the
Boa from Samoa

The Kitten from Great Britain and the Frog from Prague always enjoy a quick afternoon jog

The Kitten from Great Britain and the Grouse from Laos like to sit around the house

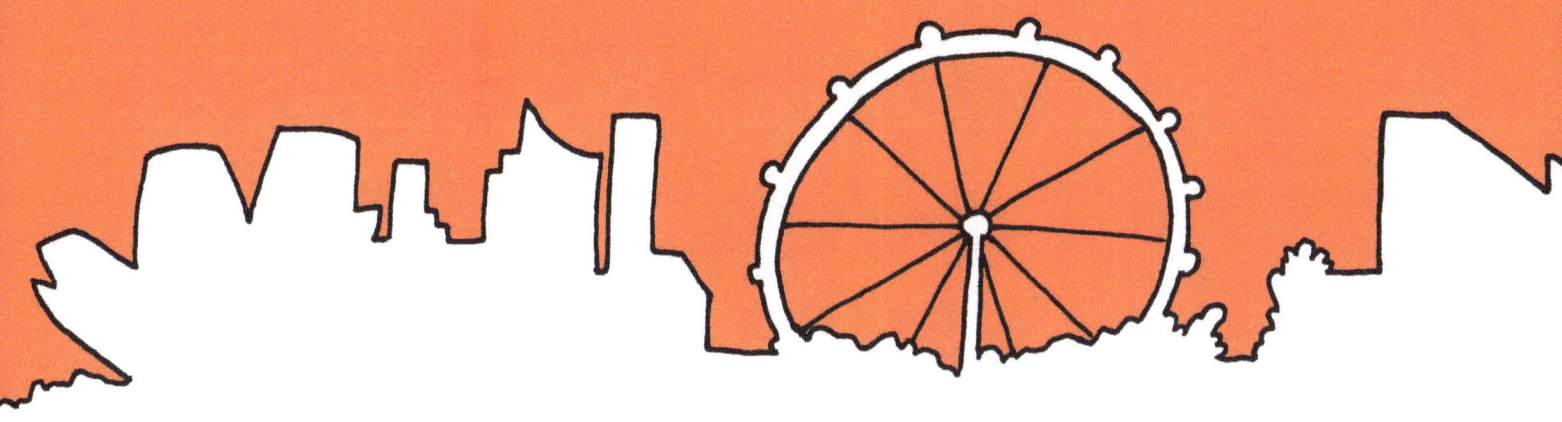

**She and the
Boar from Singapore
sing the alphabet until
the dinner table is set**

It is always fun playing Bingo with the Flamingo from Santo Domingo

The Eel from Brazil always throws dance parties with music loud enough to feel

After dark she can stargaze in pajamas with the Llama from Botswana

The Kitten from
Great Britain
loves every day

because of all the great friends with whom she can play

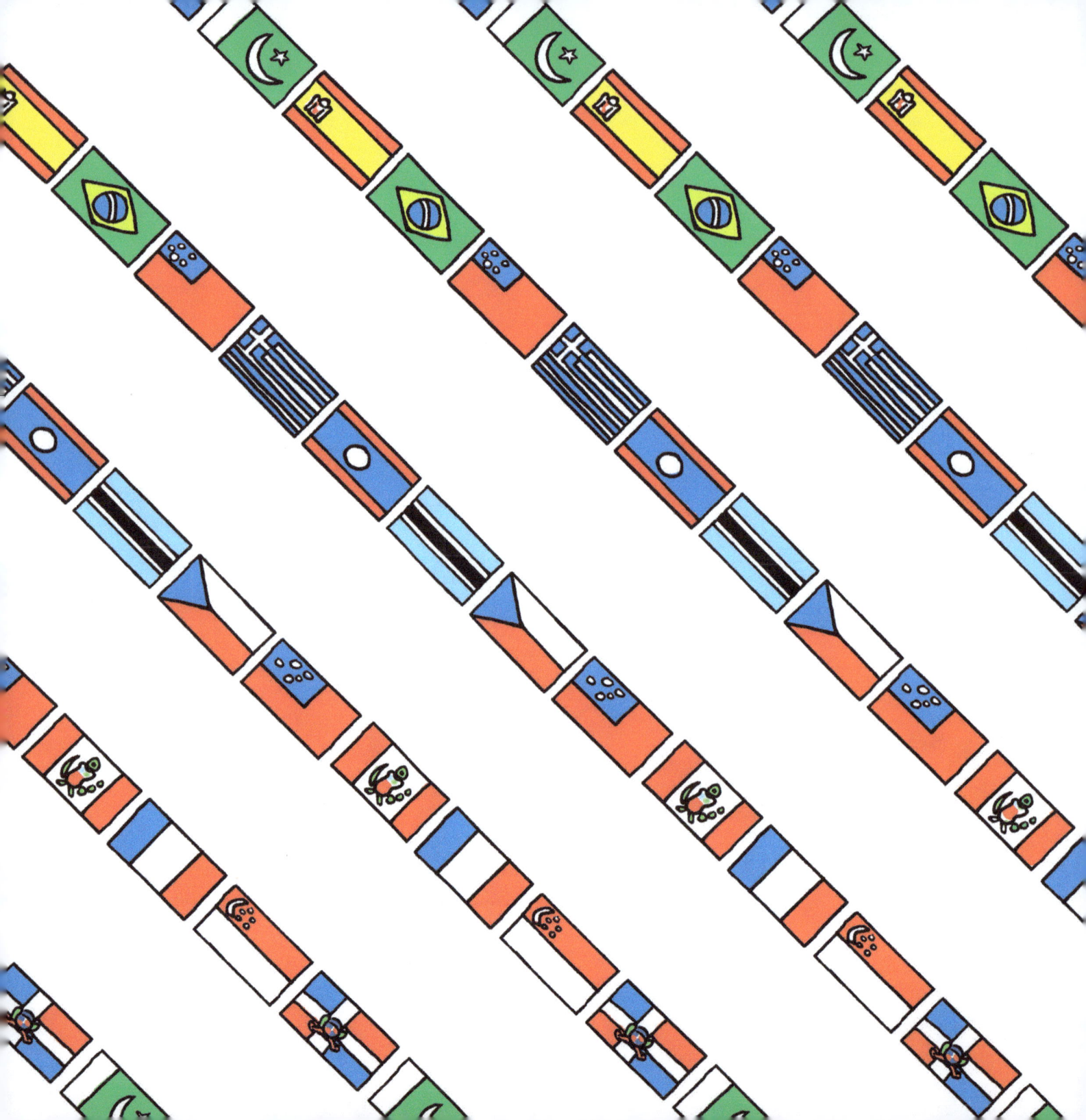

www.ingramcontent.com/pod-product-compliance
Lightning Source LLC
Chambersburg PA
CBHW041131280526
45792CB00013B/2383